HOVERING

Carol V. Davis

For Eileen Weber

In Memory of Charles Berezin z"l

Contents

Scan..3

Cauldron, Stew, Jumble 4

Shmita 5

Thinking of Water...6

Seabirds..7

Contagious..8

Dots and Dashes 9

The Fragility of the Body.............................10

Click, he says...12

Music Minus One..13

Of Course..14

Puppets, Sponges, Crayfish...........................16

The Scribe 17

Trubka..18

Merry-Go-Round...20

Between Neurons 22

Hummingbirds on the Hibiscus....................23

On the Last Day of the Year.........................24

In the Third or Fourth Year..........................25

Hovering 26

And Then...27

The Days Grow Shorter 28

Ghosts..30

Comfort..32

Anniversary 33

Acknowledgments 34

"The end is in the beginning, the ghosts shining through"

— Keetje Kuipers

Scan

I have my own room since we moved.
A bed. A desk. A dresser. A door, closed.
Refuge, though his radio
seeps through the wall, the pierce
of a trumpet or a drum startling.
His brain scan shows grey spots
like patches of fog, neurons dying,
tangles of tau proteins forming.
It's getting worse: *shoe* comes out as *shirt*
before a stream of curses explode.
Sometimes I am less than sympathetic,
tired of his anger.
Just tired.
Only the beginning.

Cauldron, Stew, Jumble

At first letters rearranged themselves
but the sentences held steady.

Then syllables unattached as if in rebellion,
the *w* and *y* tired of always being last.

A cauldron, stew of alphabet, a jumble,
where the giraffe's neck of an *f* and an *l*

broke off in class, when he was reading aloud.
That evening, he reported it, his voice

rising above a high C as panic set in.
The doctors were puzzled, shuffling him

from one expert to another, convinced
something was wrong with his eyes.

Years of medical school did not result in accuracy.
Even the hospital, always on top 10

lists of California, could not solve this.
His department chair recommended time off.

Brain scans showed a void but the 1st hospital
stuck to its eye theory. Only later when he

switched to a university, did he receive
an accurate diagnosis, so devastating that on that

Zoom (it was during Covid), he started
to cry and said he wanted to die.

But he didn't.

Shmita

This year, the 18th month
of the pandemic, is a *shmita*,
a sabbatical year, where the land
must be left fallow, any remaining
crops free for the needy.

       In the beginning,
but there isn't always one,
as now, lavender layers overlap
until darkness spreads
to every corner of the sky.

My husband tries to extract a word,
a stubborn root left for years;
it refuses to offer itself for harvest.
His once fertile mind eroding to desert.

The book of Leviticus instructs
the land must be given a rest,
its own Sabbath to replenish, but what if
a man is desperate to sow and reap,
his family dependent on these crops for survival?

How much further will my husband retreat?
In a year, will sentences disappear as when
the whale swallowed Jonah whole?

G-d promises bountiful harvests.
This month as others welcome
the new year, it is hard to celebrate.

Thinking of Water

Inching towards November
still no rain, this fifth year of drought.
My husband too is parched.
His language withering,
sometimes a drip, sometimes a deluge.
The other day he meant 'frontier,'
only it burst out as 'furniture,'
accompanied by a storm of anger.
As his abilities creak backwards,
I picture him at eight, puppy-like,
his body not yet grown into his jutting
ears, front teeth too big, with a father
who demanded to be worshipped
by everyone, even his own children,
a mother who wished she were Boston
Brahmin, not from immigrant stock.
Am I now the depository of his memories?
Our own children have taken on roles
they don't deserve: having to shave
him, take him for a walk.
A torrent of sorrow.

Seabirds

Here on a spit of land at the edge of the country,
where in college, friends and I would cross
the border for dinner, be waved through customs,

zip back to the dorms before midnight, a biologist
explains the evolution of seabirds:
the strutters, the pickers, how one beak narrowing

could extract crustaceans buried in the sand,
while another's beak broadening into a pouch
scoops fish out of the waves.

My husband, always with an opinion, is retreating,
beginning to wander in a labyrinth I cannot follow.
His path, not predictable as the tide pulsing in and out,

is punctuated by long silences one minute,
outbursts of anger the next. The doctors fluctuate
between a show of certainty, suggesting

medications not to cure but to slow,
and wavering, demonstrating too clearly
what they cannot predict.

I can't say I have the needed patience; spend
too much time dreaming of escape, longing
even for the subzero temperatures of Siberia.

Just now, the biologist points out a black
oystercatcher on an outcrop of rock, legs
covered in what looks like flesh stockings,

red beak, yellow eye rimmed red.
Its rat-a-tat-tat insistent, he stabs the air,
vigilant over the shoreline he claims.

Contagious

Not that you can catch it
but the way you are shunned
makes it seem so.

The big C (Cancer), but all
the Ds too: Divorce, Dementia.
Back up. Start with A: Alzheimer's.

Friends step away.
At first you don't notice
the signs (theirs or his),

as when a moth shuts its wings
and you think they might never
re-open. You wonder if it has died.

Only when your husband confuses
ballroom for bathroom and his boss
suggests an eye exam and a week off.

The trajectory is not an even path,
not even a cobblestone walkway,
more the jagged edges of a rocky shore.

The only certainty is the stumbling,
but who first?

Dots and Dashes

My husband invents a new language
of dots and dashes punctuated by words
mismatched to his actual demands.
Pull up the book, he exhorts, meaning
the comforter, now bunched at his feet.
A sputter of irritation
when I don't comprehend.

Later he stands, spins, pauses like
a dreidel unsure what side to land on.
The swirl of color mid-motion
lost to him: Orange, bright blue,
green of ficus leaves.
Even before the diagnosis, he could
not see the flash of color mid-twirl.
A sign something was wrong.

Nun, you get nothing, *hey* you get half.
To replenish a pile of walnuts
or pennies or nothing at all.
We'd settle for a portion.
Not what he once was,

but some semblance.
Not this shell of a man.

The Fragility of the Body

The boy broke his arm, when he tumbled out of a tree.
Next day he showed off the cast; classmates
lined up to sign it. Flowers and hearts dotted

the girls' signatures; the boys chose dark
permanent markers. Everyone surrounded Joey.
Ms. S. was forced to delay the Pledge of Allegiance.

There was room for only one kind of admiration.

Decades later, a friend fell in a parking lot.
Lucky she no longer flew as the screws, plates
and rods would set off the metal detector.

Seduction was predictably easy:
A few sweetnesses, a slight sweep
of the neck, a man's clean sheets.

The body succumbs, though the mind should
know better. How naïve I was, checking off
minimal boxes. I married, children, one, two, three.

Thanks to chance, we avoided major dangers,
even as a neighbor's son bought a gun,
disappeared on the streets, then died of an overdose.

We know the three muscles of the heart:
cardiac, smooth, skeletal, but where do
we store longing and desire?

The husband, whose gaze long focused
mostly inward, is losing connections.
His body continues, breathes in and out,

puts on weight, sleeps the required hours.
He could live like this for decades.
Posterior cortical atrophy.

The brain shrinks, so his eyes do not
see objects in front of him,
though vision can remain 20/20.

His demands multiply.
I become nothing
more than a caretaker.

No fragility to his body,
only to mine.

Click, he says

Click, he says, meaning   to button
Click, he says, meaning   to unlock
This man for whom language was   everything
is leaking words I find them on top of the dresser
      in the vegetable bin

            Think of Moses:

k'vad puh   heavy of mouth
k'vad lashon   heavy of tongue

Presented with a bowl of gold
      or one of coal
the infant reached for the gold
(proving he would usurp Pharoah)

until an angel swatted the baby's hand
      to the other bowl where he grabbed the coal
dropped it in his mouth
      burning his tongue

The stutter stayed with Moses his whole life
          *

When the cancer roared back in Smadar (my friend's
daughter)
jumbling her thoughts (she who had been a brain researcher)
      she reverted to her mother tongue until

at the end   only Hebrew dropped from her mouth
        and her husband   married 20 years
to an English speaker could not understand her

What is the future with a husband as he loses his words?

Music Minus One

Sometimes I practiced using Music Minus One:
Telemann's Trio Sonata in C Major. The harpsichord
accompaniment unflappable whenever I stumbled.

I wished the recording would pause on its own,
wait for me to catch up. Slow does not mean easy.
I learned to count in 8th notes. Challenging,

as I was never good in math. A woodwind instrument
strengthened my lungs, helping my asthma,
as I summoned the will to regulate my breath.

Now, as my husband loses words, he scrambles,
growing more and more frustrated.
My own responses speed up, irritation mounting.

"Think about the connections between the notes"
my music teacher once said. I tried to measure
the rests correctly, but I'd enter too soon or half a bar late.

My husband's speech beats a staccato rhythm,
a frantic search for what he cannot find.
A sentence minus one.

Of Course

You understand
my wish, a husband

with Alzheimer's, his demands
as numerous as pricks of light.

Once on a Petersburg night
between late fall and the threat

of first snow,
a student urged me

up a rickety wooden ladder
missing rungs, to a door

jammed shut but pushable.
We emerged onto the roof

of a pre-revolution four-story.
Streets and skyline stretched

out like branches of spruce.
This city I'd mostly traversed

underground, knew by number
of minutes between metro stops.

With no railing, the view
terrifying, too easy to step off.

Later that week, at an exhibit
of Marc Chagall's sets for the

Moscow Jewish Theater
(now an impossibility),

one canvas took up a whole wall.
The sketched man pale,

as if he knew flying from a roof
was his only chance.

This was 1921, before Chagall
himself had to flee Europe.

Now back in the United States,
I think of that figure,

wishing I too could launch
into a swirl of sky,

my own escape.

Puppets, Sponges, Crayfish

He switches fork, right hand to left and back
like a puppeteer maneuvering figures across
the stage for a performance in Central Park.
I wonder what he understands now, this man
who once lectured on the literature of resistance.
You might not notice how his mind is retreating,
only that he appears less voluble, whereas before
he dominated conversations with certainty.

I've been looking at sea sponges, classified as animals
because they don't photosynthesize but without
nervous systems or brains, more like houseplants.
No tissues or organs, their specialized cells
perform necessary functions, some in charge
of digestion, others reproduction.
Strange to do all that without a brain.
Tell me, what do we need to survive?
When the body persists but the brain does not.

Years ago, we had crayfish in a tub
on the counter, a present to the children.
One escaped; we found it clicking
across the floor, missing a limb.
Likely the cat was the culprit.
The children worried it would not survive.
It did, first it molted, then regenerated the limb.
How I wish the human brain could too.

The Scribe

Before the disease climbed into his brain,
he would hunch over a text like a *sofer*,
a Jewish scribe, checking the parchment
of the Torah, examining each letter - all 304,805.
He parsed Moby Dick, wrestling the language,
breaking down its chapters, until his students
understood how it had been assembled.
Now he scrambles his words, substituting
one for another.

Any cracks in the Torah make the scroll
pasul, unfit and unusable, until repaired
with a special pen or turkey quill.
Each tool tightly regulated:
steel, used for instruments
of death, is prohibited.

The *sofer* mends and repairs, traveling
far distances like a doctor to far-flung patients.
No cure now, only a few drugs
that might slow the progression.
The disease burrows deeper, extracting
what was important, until the brain
resembles an empty canvas,
not one with promise, but wiped clean
of any memory, of most words.

Trubka

When my husband can't summon
a word, I worry I'm losing one too.
When my 93 year old Odessan
friend says *trubka (трубка* in Cyrillic*)*
and I can't remember the English,
(though I understand the Russian),
I think, *This is it, I'm next.* I've
never met this woman (mother of a
former student), but our weekly
calls are as important to her as
to me, a conversational lifeline
to my second language. She's
stopped watching the news,
she tells me. The explosions
tear her back to the bombings
in 1941. The other day, when
she didn't answer the phone,
(*trubka*, the receiver), I feared
she was in the hospital or worse.
She's just walking slower now,
didn't make it to the phone in time.
She ends every conversation,
how glad she is to be in America.

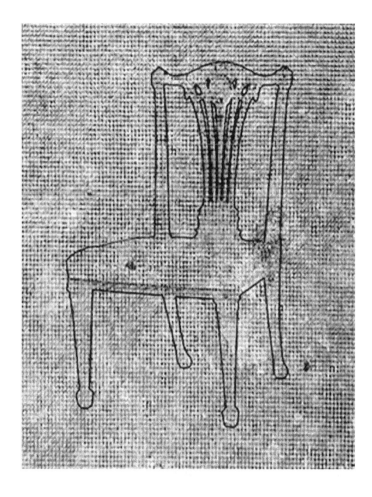

Merry-Go-Round

An 'a' and an 'r' were the first

to detach

the surrounding letters   squeezed

together so the word could be read

Soon other letters   in other words

uncoupled

like wooden animals

in a merry-go-round   breaking free from

centripetal force

and galloping through the fairgrounds

to discover what they missed those years in captivity

The English teacher managed for awhile

Students reading passages aloud

he limped to the end of the semester

until he

could no longer fool anyone

and was forced to retire

as the doctors

themselves stumbled taking months

or was it years

to diagnose what no one wanted to hear

Between Neurons

His synapses are degenerating
                a cord fraying
        a string of outdoor lights

where a bulb or two goes dark
                Connec-

                        tions
                between neurons break down

        Next, regions of the brain start to shrink

                        We are forewarned

                        Afraid of what comes next

                Time for all of us has blurred post Covid
                pre-during-not
        yet- over

        For him   the recent past is slinking away
                without designation

                        Now he recognizes me

                        In the near future
                will he encounter me
        with alarm or a blank stare?

Hummingbirds on the Hibiscus

What came first? A whir of wings
        as one hummingbird drives away the second

or a flash of color on the Rufous, an iridescent red-orange
        patch, even through the metal-laced screen door?

A bounty of pink hibiscus flowers
        claimed by the dominant bird

Thinking about ownership
        How easily it can slip out of reach

My husband is stalking words that six months ago
        he easily captured, now he grasps at them

but they have already flitted away
        Watching the hummingbirds' chase, even

with its the predictability, thrills. Maybe it's the
        maternal instinct with the birds so tiny

even insects can eat them (though usually by mistake)
        I was a patient mother

Not so much now with my husband, as my role
        changes from partner to caretaker

The heat is rising this August morning
        and the hummingbirds retreat to a shady spot

On the Last Day of the Year

In the indistinguishable hours of a nursing home day,
I push his wheelchair to an empty visiting room,
shut out the woman who churrs and chatters,
an incessant squirrel, and the man who lurches,
head down, into all the seated people
like a bumper car out of control.

Outside, house wrens, muted brown against
a winter sky, perch on nearly bare branches,
the birds' scolds a pantomime against the squirrels' taunts.
These windows will not open.
With great effort, my husband pushes himself up,
stands, feet apart, arms taut.
A victory, though it does not last.

This man whose vocabulary sent me scurrying
from breakfast table to dictionary
the decades of our marriage
has become an outline without a core.
His voice is confined to monosyllables and groans.
I too am losing track of days since he moved to the facility.
In a room with no natural light, he dwindles.
My daily phone calls shrink to minutes.
Time suspends as he diminishes.

In the Third or Fourth Year

1.

He waves his toothbrush as if it were a flag
seeking solid ground, stumbles out of the bathroom

into the hall, needing a guardrail,
the carpet now a path littered with rocks.

His hand rests on a shelf of books and commentary
though with the Alzheimer's draining his vision,

these volumes no longer bring solace.
We watch, note each small change,

fail to guess what he wants,
our responses never satisfying.

2.

In this season of repentance,
I have much to atone for:

impatience, longing to be free,
to ignore his outbursts.

This itself is a kind of bondage,
no longer a marriage.

Hovering

My husband hovers between

this world and the next

Sometimes he takes a step or two

The kids and I hold our breath willing him to pause

He rarely does

We are powerless, but I refuse

to give up   my pleas to him ever urgent   *Eat   Drink*

No turning back now

His cheekbones sharpen

as the lake beds of his cheeks empty

In my daily calls, the nurses attempt cheer

dutifully reporting how many spoonfuls and sips

When I arrive, he turns to me but what he
understands now

I cannot know

And Then

he closed his eyes.

And it was over.

The Days Grow Shorter

In death, he surfaces over and over.

Last night in a small town,
as if his appearance were normal,

we searched for food, up and down
hills, past stores that seemed open,

but weren't. When I did not know
the way, he grew increasingly agitated.

A dream tumbles without logic, maze-like,
a thoroughfare increasingly terrifying.

Turn around and roadside wildflowers
burst with color, enough for brief solace.

I wake and turn, but there is only
an indentation on the pillow,

the whiff of a man no longer there.

While alive, I rarely dreamt of him.

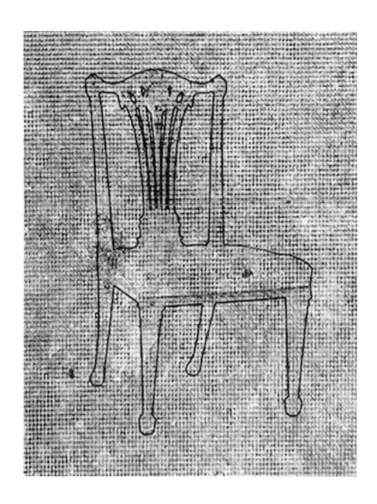

Ghosts

There is no such thing;
I know this. The way I understand
that spitting over my shoulder
to ward off the evil eye is not
effective, though I do it
to safeguard my children's health.
I cannot utter the name
of the man who hourly lies.
When he hurls another
on tv, I hear a smirk,
even though smirks
make no noise.
I glance to my left;
my husband is sitting
beside me on the couch.
The fact that he's been
dead a year has no bearing.
If anything would bring him
back from the grave, it
would be something political.
After all, we trekked first to Spain
to see the bullet holes where
Franco's army shot the partisans.
Then to Berlin where my husband
insisted on walking the path where
the communist Karl Liebknecht
was executed in Tiergarten.
Finally to visit Marx's grave in London.
As his mind slipped the last months
and his body surrendered
the will to keep going, I wondered
how much he understood.
He laughed at my anecdote

about waiters pouring soup
into Trotsky's lap when he told
the other patrons in a dairy restaurant
not to tip, that the staff
should get a living wage.
My husband did not believe
in ghosts and would have
scoffed at his reappearance now.
But it is true. I know.

Comfort

In the bottom curl of
a Treble Clef or sliding
the descending arc
of the Bass Clef.

Between half notes,
squeezed among three flats,
marking the score of a Bach Aria.
Musical shapes I once played
and now turn to for comfort.

Anniversary

A year after the death,
I plead for no more
questions about how
I am doing. No more
peering at my face,
as if the new creases
orbiting my eyes would
divulge their secrets.

Acknowledgments

My gratitude to the editors of the journals and anthology in which poems first appeared, sometimes in different versions.

Anacapa Review	"Dots and Dashes" "Music Minus One"
Atlanta Review	"Seabirds" 2024 International Poetry Contest, finalist
CCAR Journal	"Shmita"
Hamilton Stone Review	"Of Course"
I-70 Review	"Hummingbirds on the Hibiscus", "Puppets, Sponges, Crayfish"
North America Review	"Thinking of Water"
Persimmon Tree	"Scan"
Poetry South	"Trubka"
Shirim	"*Click*, he says", "The Scribe" (reprinted) "Shmita", "Thinking of Water"
Women in a Golden State Gunpowder Press, 2025	"Contagious"

I am grateful to the UCLA Alzheimer's and Dementia Care Program and its support group. And to Los Angeles Jewish Health. A special thank you to Andrea Carter Brown, my first reader for many of these poems. To my communities, immense gratitude for the before, during and after. And to friends who were there when I most needed it. As always to David and Colleen, Bernie, Jacob and Teddy. Thank you to Brad Freeman for the cover art and to Brian Jacobs at Tofu Ink Arts Press for giving these poems a home.

Carol V. Davis is the author of *Below Zero*, (Stephen F. Austin State University Press, 2023), *Because I Cannot Leave This Body* (Truman State Univ. Press, 2017) and *Between Storms* (TSUP, 2012). She won the 2007 T.S. Eliot Prize for *Into the Arms of Pushkin: Poems of St. Petersburg. It's Time to Talk About...* was published in Russia, in a bilingual English/Russian edition (Symposium, 1997). Her poetry has been read on National Public Radio, the Library of Congress and Radio Russia. Twice a Fulbright scholar in Russia, 1996-97 and 2005, she taught in Siberia, winters 2017 and 2018 and teaches at Santa Monica College, California and Antioch University Los Angeles. She was awarded a Fulbright Specialist grant for Siberia in 2020, postponed because of Covid restrictions and now cancelled.